The CoinHub

An Ultimate Guide to Coin Errors

BLAKE ALMA

TABLE OF CONTENTS:

INTRODUCTION: WHAT'S THE ERROR? INTRODUCTION TO US COIN ERRORS

Welcome to the CoinHub, a journey into the fascinating world of US coin errors. Have you ever taken a closer look at your pocket change and noticed something peculiar? Those quirks and mistakes in the coin-making process are what we're here to explore. From minor deviations to major structural anomalies, coin errors make for a thrilling addition to any coin collection and can even hold significant value. As an avid collector and the founder of CoinHub Media, I invite you to join me as we delve deep into the stories behind these intriguing coins and discover the excitement they hold.

Importance of Coin Errors

Coin errors are more than just mistakes. They offer a unique window into the coin-making process and the technology available at the time. Throughout history, coin errors have been a source of fascination for collectors and have played an important role in the numismatic market

Overview of the US Coin Error Market

The market for coin errors is constantly evolving, and new and exciting errors are discovered every year. As more collectors become interested in these unique coins, the market for coin errors continues to grow and offers a diverse range of opportunities for collectors at all levels. Whether you're a seasoned collector or just starting out, the US coin error market has something for everyone.

So, there you have it, folks! A brief introduction to the wild and wacky world of US coin errors. Who knows, you might just have a valuable error hiding in your change jar!

CHAPTER 1: THE WILD WORLD OF COIN ERRORS: TYPES AND THEIR STORIES

Welcome to the exciting world of American coin errors! In this chapter, we'll explore the different types of errors that can occur during the coin-making process. From struck through errors to double dies, every error has a unique story to tell. So, grab a magnifying glass and let's dive in!

Mint Errors

These are errors that occur during the striking process. Here are a few of the most common mint errors:

- Off-Center Strikes: These are coins that have been struck off-center, resulting in part of the design missing. It's like the coin decided to take a break from the standard design.

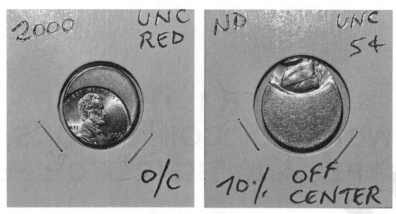

Off Centered Strikes

- Double Struck Coins: These are coins that have been struck twice, resulting in a doubled image. It's like the coin wanted to make sure its image was really imprinted!

Double Struck Examples

- Clipped Planchets: These are coins that have had a portion of the planchet cut off, resulting in a missing part of the design. It's like the coin lost a piece of itself.

Clipped planchet

Die Errors: These are errors that occur during the die-making process. Here are a few of the most common die errors:

- Die Breaks: These are coins that have a broken die, resulting in a raised line on the coin. It's like the die got tired and took a break.
- Die Cracks: These are coins that have a cracked die, resulting in a raised line on the coin. It's like the die took a hit and couldn't handle it.

Die Crack on a 2021 Penny "Spiked Head Error"

3

- Double Die: These are coins that have a doubled image due to a die that was not properly aligned. It's like the die wanted to make sure its image was really imprinted. We will talk a lot about this later.
- Mechanical Doubling: These are coins that have a doubled image due to a mechanical issue during the striking process.
- Strike-Through Errors: These are coins that have foreign objects such as hair, fibers, or grease become trapped between the die and planchet during the striking process, resulting in unique and often eye-catching variations on the coin's surface.

Strike Through error on a 2005 Kansas quarter "In God We Rust"

- Die chips: These are small defects on coins caused by a piece of the metal die breaking off during minting. They result in unintended marks or raised areas on the coin's surface. These mint errors can sometimes add value for collectors, depending on their size, location, and rarity.

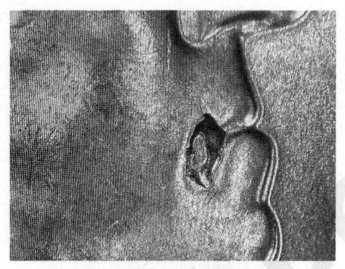

Die chip on a 2022 quarter

- Die Gouges: These are coins that have a gouge in the die, resulting in a raised line on the coin. It's like the die got a scar and wanted to show it off.

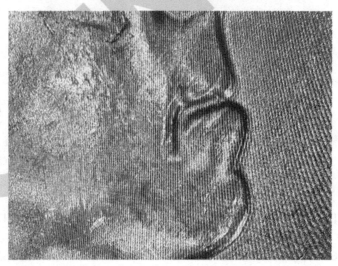

Die gouge on a 2022 quarter

Planchet Errors: These are errors that occur during the planchet-making process. Here are a few of the most common planchet errors:

- Lamination Errors: These are coins that have a flaked piece of metal, resulting in a missing part of the design. It's like the coin lost a piece of itself.

Lamination error on a 1902 Barber quarter

- Improperly Annealed Planchets: These are coins that have not been properly annealed, resulting in a weak or brittle planchet. It's like the coin was born with a flaw.
- Blank planchet errors: These coins are caused by the accidental omission of the design on the coin.

The beginning tour through the exciting world of US coin errors. The next time you're handling coins, take a closer look and see if you can spot any errors. You never know what treasure you might find!

CHAPTER 2: THE ART OF DETECTION: HOW TO IDENTIFY COIN ERRORS

You've got a roll of coins in hand and a glint of excitement in your eye. You're ready to search for those rare and valuable coin errors. But, how do you know if you've found one? That's where the art of detection comes in. In this chapter, we'll explore the tools and techniques you can use to identify coin errors.

Visual Inspection

The first step in identifying coin errors is to take a good look at the coin. Use your naked eye to inspect the coin for any deviations from the standard design. If you see anything that looks unusual, it's time to break out the magnifying glass.

Magnification

A magnifying glass is your best friend when it comes to identifying coin errors. It will help you see the details of the coin and identify any deviations from the standard design. Whether you use a hand-held magnifying glass, loupe, or a microscope, the goal is to get a closer look at the coin and see what you can find.

Good Microscopes for Coin Error Hunting

If you're serious about finding coin errors, a microscope can be a valuable tool. When choosing a microscope for coin error hunting, look for one with high magnification and good clarity. Some popular options for coin collectors include stereo microscopes and digital microscopes. Do your research and choose the microscope that best fits your needs and budget.

Coin Grading

Coin grading is the process of evaluating a coin's condition and assigning it a numerical grade. This is a useful tool for identifying coin errors because it will help you determine the rarity and value of the coin. Whether you use a professional grading service (like NGC) or do it yourself, the goal is to get a better understanding of the coin's condition and value.

The tools and techniques you need to identify coin errors. So, grab your magnifying glass, put on your detective hat, and start searching for those rare and valuable errors!

The ABCs of Coin Grading: Understanding the Grading Scale

Coin grading is an important tool for identifying the rarity and value of coin errors. But what exactly is coin grading and how does it work? In this subchapter, we'll explore the basics of coin grading and the grading scale.

What is Coin Grading?

Coin grading is the process of evaluating a coin's condition and assigning it a numerical grade. This grade reflects the coin's overall appearance, including its strike, luster, and surface preservation. The higher the grade, the better the condition of the coin.

The Grading Scale

The grading scale for coins ranges from 1 to 70, with 70 being the highest grade possible. The most commonly used grading scale is the Sheldon Scale, which was developed by Dr. William Sheldon in the 1950s. Here's a brief overview of the Sheldon Scale:

- 1-49: Poor to Fair: These coins are heavily worn and show significant damage.
- AU 50-59: About Uncirculated: Coins in this range may have very slight wear on the high points of the design, but the overall details and luster are still quite strong.
- MS 60 - Mint State 60: A coin in MS 60 grade shows moderate wear and tear, but the overall design and lettering are still clearly visible.
- MS 63 - Mint State 63: A coin in MS 63 grade shows light wear, with slight flattening of the highest points, but still retains much of its original luster.
- MS 65 - Mint State 65: A coin in MS 65 grade has light wear and retains much of its original luster, but may have a few small marks or nicks.
- MS 70 - A coin in 70 grade is considered a perfect coin, with no visible marks or hairlines and an excellent strike.

That is basics of coin grading and the grading scale. Whether you're a seasoned collector or just starting out, understanding the grading scale is an important tool for identifying the rarity and value of coin errors.

CHAPTER 3: HOW MUCH IS THAT ERROR? THE VALUE OF COIN ERRORS

So, you've found a coin error and you're wondering what it's worth. Well, buckle up, because it's time to explore CoinHub's world of coin error values! In this chapter, we'll take a look at the factors that affect the value of coin errors and how to estimate their worth.

Factors that Affect Value

The value of coin errors is determined by a number of factors, including rarity, condition, and popularity. Let's take a closer look:

Rarity: The rarer the error, the more valuable it is. It's simple supply and demand. If there are only a handful of a certain error in existence, it's going to be worth more than one that's more common. For example, a rare double die error might be worth hundreds or even thousands of dollars, while a more common error like a clipped planchet might only be worth a few dollars.

Condition: The condition of the error is another important factor in determining its value. A coin that's in pristine condition is going to be worth more than one that's heavily worn or damaged. The condition of the coin is often referred to as its "grade," and coins are typically assigned a grade on a scale of 1 to 70, with 70 being the highest grade possible. For example, a coin that's in perfect condition and has been graded as "70" is going to be worth more than a coin that's heavily worn and has been graded as "10".

Popularity: The popularity of the error is also a factor in determining its value. If a certain error is in high demand among collectors, it's going to be worth more than one that's less sought after. For example, a rare double-die error might be worth thousands of dollars if it's popular among collectors, while a less popular error like a die break might only be worth a few dollars.

Estimating the Value of a Coin Error

So, how do you estimate the value of a coin error? The best way is to consult a professional coin dealer or use a coin price guide (like the Redbook). These resources will give you a good idea of the value of the error based on its rarity, condition, and popularity. You can also have the coin professionally graded by a coin grading service like NGC, which will provide a more accurate estimate of the coin's value.

It's important to keep in mind that the value of coin errors can fluctuate over time based on changes in supply and demand. For example, the popularity of a certain error might increase, causing its value to rise, or a new discovery of a similar error might increase the supply, causing its value to fall.

This is the value of coin errors in a nutshell. Whether you're looking to add to your collection or just curious, understanding the factors that affect the value of these unique coins is an important part of the hobby. So, put on your detective hat and start exploring the exciting world of coin errors!

CHAPTER 4: THE THRILL OF THE HUNT! COLLECTING COIN ERRORS

So, you've been bitten by the coin error bug and you're ready to start your own collection. Congratulations! Collecting coin errors is a fun and exciting hobby that can bring you years of enjoyment. In this chapter, we'll take a look at the ins and outs of collecting coin errors, including how to build a collection, store and display your coins, and protect your investment.

Building a Collection

Building a collection of coin errors is a journey, not a destination. To get started, you'll need to set some goals, build a budget, and find reliable dealers. Let's take a closer look:

Setting Goals: What do you want to get out of your coin error collection? Do you want to focus on a specific type of error, like off-center strikes? Or do you want to build a diverse collection that includes a variety of errors? Setting clear goals will help you stay focused and make the most of your collection. You might also consider setting a goal for the number of coins you want to have in your collection or the types of errors you want to include.

Building a Budget: Building a collection of coin errors can be an expensive hobby, so it's important to have a budget in place. This will help you avoid overspending and ensure that you're able to purchase the coins you really want. You might consider setting a monthly or yearly budget for your collection, or you might set aside a portion of your income each month to buy coins.

Finding Reliable Dealers: Finding reliable dealers is key to building a successful coin error collection. Look for dealers who have a good reputation, specialize in coin errors, and offer a return policy. This will help you avoid scams and ensure that you're getting the real deal. You might also consider attending coin shows or joining a coin club to connect with other collectors and dealers.

Storing and Displaying Coin Errors

Once you've started your collection, it's important to store and display your coins properly to protect their value. Consider using protective holders and keeping your coins in a safe, secure location. You might also consider displaying your coins in a coin album or on a coin stand to show off your collection to friends and family. If you plan on displaying your coins, be sure to choose a location that is free from extreme temperatures, humidity, and direct sunlight, which can cause damage to your coins over time.

Protecting Your Collection

Protecting your collection is an important part of collecting coin errors. Consider insuring your collection to protect it against theft or damage. You might also consider using a safe deposit box or home safe to keep your coins secure. You can also take steps to protect your collection by avoiding handling your coins too much and storing them in a dry, cool place.

The Big No-No

As a coin collector, you might be tempted to clean your coins to make them look shiny and new. However, this is a big mistake.

Cleaning your coins will actually harm their value and make them less attractive to other collectors. Here's why:

Removes Patina: Patina is the natural toning that occurs on coins over time. It is a sign of age and history and is highly valued by collectors. When you clean your coins, you remove the patina and erase the coin's history. This can significantly decrease the coin's value.

Damages the Surface: Cleaning coins can also damage the surface of the coin. Abrasive cleaning methods can scratch the coin, while harsh chemicals can remove the metal or change the color of the coin. This type of damage is permanent and can never be undone.

Decreases Authenticity: Coins that have been cleaned are often considered less authentic. A coin's authenticity is an important factor in its value and cleaning it can make it appear as if the coin has been altered or tampered with.

Creates Uniformity: Cleaning coins can create uniformity and remove any unique characteristics that make the coin special. Coins with unique toning, spots, or other natural imperfections are highly valued by collectors, as they add to the coin's story and history.

So, what should you do instead of cleaning your coins? The best course of action is to simply leave them as they are. If you want to protect your coins from further damage, you can store them properly in coin holders or albums. You can also have a professional coin dealer or grading service examine your coins to determine their value and authenticity.

In short, cleaning your coins is a big no-no in the world of coin collecting. Don't let the temptation to make your coins look shiny and new harm their value. Embrace the natural patina and unique characteristics that make your coins special, and watch their value grow over time.

CHAPTER 5: THE HUNT IS ON! COIN ROLL HUNTING

Coin roll hunting is a fun and exciting way to search for coin errors. It involves searching through rolls of coins, often purchased from a bank, to find coins with errors or other unique features. In this chapter, we'll explore the ins and outs of coin roll hunting, including what to look for, how to get started, and tips for making the most of your hunt.

What to Look For

Coin roll hunting is all about finding coins with errors or other unique features. Some common errors to look for include off-center strikes, double-struck coins, and clipped planchets. You might also find coins with die errors, such as die breaks, die chips, or double dies. When coin roll hunting, it's important to have a good eye and a keen attention to detail.

How to Get Started

To get started with coin roll hunting, you'll need to purchase rolls of coins from a bank. You might also consider searching through your own spare change or asking friends and family to save their change for you. When you have a roll of coins, take your time to inspect each coin carefully, using a magnifying glass or other tool if needed. If you find a coin with an error, be sure to set it aside and continue your search.

Tips for Making the Most of Your Hunt

To make the most of your coin roll hunting experience, consider the following tips:

Start with fresh rolls: Fresh federally wrapped rolls of coins from the bank are more likely to contain errors or unique coins.

Be patient: Coin roll hunting can be time-consuming, but it's important to take your time and inspect each coin carefully.

Use the right tools: A magnifying glass, coin loupe, or other tool can help you see details more clearly and make it easier to find errors.

Join a coin club: Joining a coin club, like a coin-related Facebook group, can be a great way to connect with other collectors and learn more about coin roll hunting.

Keep a record of your finds: Keeping a record of your coin roll hunting finds can help you track your progress and keep your collection organized.

Coin roll hunting is a fun and exciting way to search for coin errors. Whether you're just starting out or a seasoned collector, this hobby offers a lifetime of excitement and satisfaction. So, grab your magnifying glass, head to the bank, and start your next coin roll hunting adventure!

CHAPTER 6: THE INSIDE SCOOP! UNDERSTANDING MINT MARKS AND THE ANATOMY OF A COIN

To truly appreciate the unique features of coin errors, it's important to understand the significance of mint marks and the anatomy of a coin. In this chapter, we'll dive deeper into these concepts and give you all the inside information you need to understand what makes coins so special.

Mint Marks

Mint marks are tiny symbols or letters found on coins that indicate the mint where the coin was produced. The United States has had several mints throughout its history, each with its own distinct mint mark. The mint marks serve as a way to identify the origin of the coin and to distinguish it from coins produced at other mints.

Here are some of the most common mint marks and the mints they represent:

- "P": Philadelphia Mint, the oldest mint in the United States, established in 1792.
- "S": San Francisco Mint, established in 1854.

- "D": Denver Mint, established in 1906.
- "W": West Point Mint, established in 1988.

It's worth noting that not all coins have mint marks, as some coins, such as those produced at the Philadelphia Mint before 1980, do not have them. However, many coins, especially modern issues, do carry mint marks, and they can be a valuable tool for collectors and enthusiasts alike.

The Anatomy of a Coin

To fully understand the unique features of coin errors, it's essential to know the basic anatomy of a coin. Here's a closer look at the key components of a typical coin:

Obverse: The obverse is the front side of the coin and typically features a portrait of a historical figure, such as George Washington or Abraham Lincoln.

Reverse: The reverse is the back side of the coin and often features a design related to the theme of the coin, such as an eagle, a shield, or a building.

Rim: The rim is the raised edge of the coin that helps protect the design from wear and tear.

Edge: The edge of the coin is the part that runs around the circumference of the coin and can be smooth, reeded, or have other designs, such as lettered edges or ornate borders.

Field: The field is the flat surface of the coin between the rim and the design. On many coins, the field is blank and serves as a background for the design, but on some coins, it may also feature inscriptions or other elements.

In conclusion, understanding the significance of mint marks and the anatomy of a coin is essential for appreciating the unique features of coin errors. Whether you're just starting out or a seasoned collector, this information will help you understand what makes coins so special and how to best appreciate the errors and anomalies that make them so fascinating.

CHAPTER 7: A CENTURY OF COINS - A LOOK AT THE HISTORY AND FUN FACTS OF COINS

In the last hundred years, the United States has produced a wide variety of coins, each with its own unique history and story. In this chapter, we'll delve deeper into the history and designs of some of the most interesting and important coins produced in the last century (give or take) and explore the fun facts behind each one.

The Lincoln Cent

The Lincoln cent was first introduced in 1909 to commemorate the 100th anniversary of Abraham Lincoln's birth. This coin features a portrait of Lincoln on the obverse and two wheat stalks on the reverse. The design of the Lincoln cent has undergone several changes over the years, offering a unique window into the history of coin production.

The Wheat Cent Design (1909-1958): The original design of the Lincoln cent featured a portrait of Lincoln on the obverse and two wheat stalks on the reverse. This design, which was in use for nearly 50 years, is now referred to as the Wheat cent.

Wheat Cent (Images provided by Numismatic
Guaranty Company - NGC)

The Lincoln Memorial Design (1959-2008): In 1959, the design of the Lincoln cent was changed to commemorate the 150th anniversary of Lincoln's birth. The obverse design now featured a bust of Lincoln, while the reverse featured a depiction of the Lincoln Memorial. This design was in use for nearly 50 years and remains a favorite among collectors.

Lincoln memorial cent (Images provided by
Numismatic Guaranty Company - NGC)

The Bicentennial Design (2009): In 2009, the design of the Lincoln cent was changed again to commemorate the 200th anniversary of Lincoln's birth. The obverse design featured a bust of Lincoln, while the reverse featured four different designs, each reflecting a different aspect of Lincoln's life and legacy. These designs included a log cabin, Lincoln as a young man reading, Lincoln as a statesman, and Lincoln as the president.

2009 Lincoln bicentennial cents (Images provided
by Numismatic Guaranty Company - NGC)

The Shield Cent Design (2010-present): In 2010, the design of the Lincoln cent was changed once again to a new design featuring a shield on the reverse. This design was meant to symbolize the strength and unity of the country and remains in use today.

Union shield cent (Images provided by
Numismatic Guaranty Company - NGC)

The Buffalo Nickel

The Buffalo nickel was first introduced in 1913 and features the image of a buffalo on the obverse and a Native American on the reverse. This coin was in circulation for just 25 years, but it remains a favorite among collectors. The obverse design features a portrait of a Native American, while the reverse design features a buffalo, which was meant to symbolize the rugged frontier spirit of the American West. Did you know that the Buffalo nickel was designed by James Earle Fraser, who drew inspiration from real-life buffalo and Native American models?

Buffalo nickel (Images provided by Numismatic
Guaranty Company - NGC)

The Jefferson Nickel

The Jefferson nickel was first introduced in 1938 and replaced the Buffalo nickel. This coin features a portrait of Thomas Jefferson on the obverse and his home, Monticello, on the reverse. The design of the Jefferson nickel has undergone several changes over the years, offering a unique window into the history of coin production.

The Original Jefferson Nickel Design (1938-2004): The original design of the Jefferson nickel featured a portrait of Jefferson on the obverse and a depiction of Monticello on the reverse. This design was in use for over 60 years.

Original Jefferson nickel (Images provided by Numismatic Guaranty Company - NGC)

Silver War Nickels: The Silver War Nickels were a special type of nickel produced during World War II, from 1942 to 1945. These nickels were made of a silver-copper alloy and were designed to conserve nickel, which was in short supply due to the war effort.

Silver war nickel – the mint mark was temporarily
placed above the Monticello building (Images provided
by Numismatic Guaranty Company - NGC)

The Westward Journey Series (2004-2005): In 2004, the design
of the Jefferson nickel was changed as part of the Westward
Journey Series. This series consisted of two designs, each
reflecting a different aspect of Jefferson's life and legacy. The first
design featured a depiction of Jefferson crossing the Potomac
River, while the second design featured a depiction of Lewis and
Clark's expedition.

The Westward Journey nickel series (Source: Smyrna Coins)

Modified Jefferson (2006-present): In 2006, the design of the Jefferson nickel was changed back to Jefferson's bust but facing forward, featuring the same depiction of Monticello on the reverse. This design remains in use today.

Modified Jefferson nickel (Images provided by Numismatic Guaranty Company - NGC)

The Roosevelt Dime

The Roosevelt Dime was first minted in 1946 to honor President Franklin D. Roosevelt following his passing. The obverse of the coin features a portrait of Roosevelt. On the reverse, there is a torch symbolizing liberty, an olive branch for peace, and an oak branch for strength and independence. Interestingly, the Roosevelt Dime was the first US coin to feature a president shortly after his death.

The Roosevelt Dime (Images provided by
Numismatic Guaranty Company - NGC)

The Washington Quarter

The Washington quarter was first introduced in 1932 to commemorate the 200th anniversary of George Washington's birth.
This coin features a portrait of Washington on the obverse and
an eagle on the reverse. The design of the Washington quarter
has undergone several changes over the years, offering a unique
window into the history of coin production.

The Original Washington Quarter Design (1932-1998): The
original design of the Washington quarter featured a portrait of
Washington on the obverse and an eagle on the reverse. This
design was in use for over 60 years and remains a very popular
choice among collectors.

The original Washington quarter (Images provided
by Numismatic Guaranty Company - NGC)

The State Quarters Program (1999-2008): In 1999, the design
of the Washington quarter was changed as part of the State
Quarters Program. This program allowed each state to select a
design that reflected its unique history, culture, and landmarks.
The obverse design remained mostly the same, featuring a portrait of Washington, while the reverse design changed to reflect
each state's chosen design.

The National Park Quarters Program (2010-2021): In 2010, the
design of the Washington quarter was changed again as part of the
National Park Quarters Program. This program allowed each state
to select a design that reflected one of its national parks or other
sites of national interest. The obverse design remained the same,
featuring a portrait of Washington, while the reverse design changed
to reflect each state's chosen park or site.

The 2021 Crossing the Delaware Quarter: In 2021, the
Washington quarter design was temporarily changed to commemorate the anniversary of George Washington's famous crossing
of the Delaware River. The obverse design remained the same
as the original design, featuring a portrait of Washington, while
the reverse design featured an image of Washington crossing the
Delaware River with his troops.

Crossing the Delaware quarter (Images provided
by Numismatic Guaranty Company - NGC)

The American Women Quarters Program (2022-present): In
2022, the design of the Washington quarter was changed again
as part of the American Women Quarters Program. This program is dedicated to honoring the contributions and achievements of American women throughout history. The obverse
design changed but still featuring a portrait of Washington, while
the reverse design changes to reflect the chosen woman being
honored.

The Kennedy Half Dollar

The Kennedy half dollar was first introduced in 1964, just a year
after President John F. Kennedy was assassinated. The obverse
design features a bust of Kennedy, while the reverse design features the Presidential Seal, which was meant to symbolize the
authority and power of the presidency.

Kennedy half dollar (Images provided by
Numismatic Guaranty Company - NGC)

Dollar Coins

The dollar coin has a rich history, with several different designs and denominations being produced over the last few decades. Dollar coins offer a unique window into the history and evolution of coin production.

The Eisenhower Dollar (1971-1978): The Eisenhower dollar (aka the Ike dollar) was introduced in 1971 to commemorate the life and legacy of President Dwight D. Eisenhower. This coin features a portrait of Eisenhower on the obverse and an eagle landing on the moon on the reverse. The Eisenhower dollar was in circulation until 1978.

Proof Eisenhower dollar (Images provided by
Numismatic Guaranty Company - NGC)

The Susan B. Anthony Dollar (1979-1981, 1999): The Susan B. Anthony dollar was introduced in 1979 to commemorate the life and legacy of suffragist Susan B. Anthony. This coin features a portrait of Anthony on the obverse and an eagle on the reverse. The Susan B. Anthony dollar was in circulation from 1979 to 1981 and was re-introduced in 1999 for a limited time.

Susan B. Anthony dollar (Images provided by
Numismatic Guaranty Company - NGC)

The Native American $1 Coin (also known as the "Golden Dollar"): The Native American $1 Coin was introduced in 2000 as part of the Native American $1 Coin Program. This program is dedicated to honoring the contributions and achievements of Native Americans throughout history. The Native American $1 Coin is golden in color and made of a manganese-brass composition, making it easily distinguishable from other coins.

Native American dollar (Images provided by
Numismatic Guaranty Company - NGC)

The Presidential $1 Coin Program (2007-2016): The Presidential $1 Coin Program was introduced in 2007 to honor the former Presidents of the United States in the order that they served. The obverse of the coin features a portrait of the President, while the reverse features a depiction of the Statue of Liberty. The Presidential $1 Coin Program is an ongoing series, and new coins are released each year to commemorate the Presidents who served in office.

Proof Roosevelt dollar (Images provided by
Numismatic Guaranty Company - NGC)

CHAPTER 8: COINS THAT EVERY COLLECTOR SHOULD KNOW ABOUT

Welcome to CoinHub's list of coin errors that every collector should be familiar with. This is the part you have been waiting for! I want to thank the Numismatic Guaranty Company (NGC) for providing us with photos to visually illustrate some of the errors we'll be discussing.

Say no more, here is our list of coin errors!

Pennies

- 1942-D OVER HORIZONTAL D - A penny produced at the Denver Mint in 1942 with a portion of the "D" mint mark stamped over a horizontal "D."

1942-D OVER HORIZONTAL D (Images provided by Numismatic Guaranty Company - NGC)

- 1943-D BRONZE – This penny is one of the most famous and valuable coins in U.S. numismatic history, as it was struck in error during a time when pennies were supposed to be made from zinc-coated steel due to copper shortages during World War II.

1943-D bronze penny (Images provided by
Numismatic Guaranty Company - NGC)

- 1944 STEEL - A penny produced at the Philadelphia Mint in 1944 accidently made of steel due to a copper shortage the year before, with a small number of steel planchets mistakenly used.

1944 steel penny (Images provided by
Numismatic Guaranty Company - NGC)

- 1944 D OVER S - A penny produced at the Denver Mint in 1944 with a portion of the "D" mint mark stamped over an "S."

1944 D over S penny (Images provided by Numismatic Guaranty Company - NGC)

- 1945-S MICRO S - A penny produced at the San Francisco Mint in 1945 with a smaller than usual "S" mint mark.

1945 S over micro S (Images provided by Numismatic Guaranty Company - NGC)

- 1948-S OVER D - A penny produced at the San Francisco Mint in 1948 with a portion of the "S" mint mark stamped over a "D."

- 1955 DOUBLED-DIE - A penny produced at the Philadelphia Mint in 1955 with a double-struck die, resulting in a coin with two images.

1955 double-die penny (Images provided by Numismatic Guaranty Company - NGC)

- 1958 DDO - A penny produced at the Denver Mint in 1958 with a doubled die, resulting in a coin with two images.

1958 double-die penny (Images provided by Numismatic Guaranty Company - NGC)

- 1969-D NO FG – A penny that is missing the initials "FG" on the reverse. This occurs when the die that stamps the coin fails to strike the designer's initials due to grease caught in the die.

This 1969-D penny is missing the designer's initials. (Images provided by Numismatic Guaranty Company - NGC)

- 1969-S DOUBLED-DIE - A penny produced at the San Francisco Mint in 1969 with a double-struck die, resulting in a coin with two images.

1969-S double-die penny (Images provided by Numismatic Guaranty Company - NGC)

- 1970-S SMALL DATE - A penny produced at the San Francisco Mint in 1970 with a smaller than usual date.

1970-S large date (left) & 1970-S small date (right) Notice how the "7" doesn't extend pass the "0" on the small date. (Images provided by Numismatic Guaranty Company - NGC)

- 1972 DOUBLED DIE - A penny produced at the Philadelphia Mint in 1972 with a double-struck die, resulting in a coin with two images.

1972 double-die penny (Images provided by Numismatic Guaranty Company - NGC)

- 1972-D DOUBLED DIE - A penny produced at the Denver Mint in 1972 with a double-struck die, resulting in a coin with two images.
- 1983 DDR DOUBLE-DIE - A penny produced at the Philadelphia Mint in 1983 with a double-struck die, resulting in a coin with two images.
- 1984 DOUBLE EAR - A penny produced at the Philadelphia Mint in 1984 with two distinct earlobes on the image of Lincoln on the obverse.

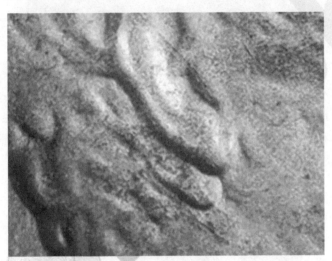

1984 double ear penny. (Images provided by
Numismatic Guaranty Company - NGC)

- 1984 D DDO and 1987 D/D pennies - Pennies produced at the Denver Mint in their respective years with doubled designs, resulting in a second, slightly offset image.
- 1992 CLOSE AM - A penny produced at the Philadelphia Mint in 1992 with the "AM" in "AMERICA" on the reverse closer together than normal.

1992 Close AM penny. (Images provided by
Numismatic Guaranty Company - NGC)

- 1994 DOUBLE COLUMN – - A penny produced at the Philadelphia Mint in 1994 that doubling on the reverse side of the coin. The error makes it appear as if the far right column is doubled.

1994 double column penny (Images provided by
Numismatic Guaranty Company - NGC)

- 1998, 1999, 2000 WIDE AM - Pennies produced at the Philadelphia Mint in 1998 - 2000 with a wider than usual "AM" in "AMERICA" on the reverse.

Wide AM penny (Images provided by Numismatic
Guaranty Company - NGC)

- 2004 (DDR), 2006 (DDO) and 2014 (DDO) DOUBLE DIE -
  Pennies produced at the Philadelphia Mint with a doubled
  design, resulting in a second, slightly offset image.

2006 double-die penny (Images provided by
Numismatic Guaranty Company - NGC)

2014 double-die penny (Images provided by
Numismatic Guaranty Company - NGC)

Nickels

- 1938 DDO - This error occurs when the design on the obverse side of the nickel is doubled, resulting in a second, slightly offset image.

1938 double-die nickel (Images provided by Numismatic Guaranty Company - NGC)

- 1938 QDO - This error occurs when the obverse design is quadrupled, creating four images of the design on the same side of the coin.

1938 quadruple die nickel (Images provided by Numismatic Guaranty Company - NGC)

- 1939 REV OF 38 and 1939 REV OF 40 - These errors occur when the reverse design of the previous year's nickel is used instead of the current year's design.

1939 reverse of 1938 (Images provided by
Numismatic Guaranty Company - NGC)

- 1940 S/S (Small and Large S) - This error occurs when
  two different size mint marks are used on the same coin.

1940 S over S (Images provided by Numismatic
Guaranty Company - NGC)

- 1942 DDO - This error occurs when the obverse design is doubled, creating a second, offset image.
- 1942 P/P - This error occurs when two punches are used to create the mint mark, resulting in a double image.

1942 P over P nickel (Images provided by Numismatic Guaranty Company - NGC)

- 1946 DDR - This error occurs when the reverse design is doubled, creating a second, offset image.
- 1946 D/INVERT D - This error occurs when the mint mark is inverted and doubled, appearing upside down.

1946 D over inverted D nickel (Images provided by Numismatic Guaranty Company - NGC)

- 1949 D/S - This error occurs when the D and S mint marks overlap.
- 1951 DDO - This error occurs when the obverse design is doubled, creating a second, offset image.
- 1953 D/INVERT D - This nickel was made at the Denver Mint in 1953 and has an error where the "D" mint mark is doubled with the second "D" being upside down.
- 1954 D/D - This nickel was made at the Denver Mint in 1954 and has an error where the "D" mint mark was stamped over a "D".
- 1954 S/D - This nickel was made at the San Francisco Mint in 1954 and has an error where the "S" mint mark was stamped over a "D".
- 1954 S/S - This nickel was made at the San Francisco Mint in 1954 and has an error where the "S" mint mark was stamped over a "S".
- 1954 S DDR - This nickel has an error called "Doubled Die Reverse". This means that the back side of the nickel was struck twice, creating a double image.

1954-S double die reverse nickel (Images provided by Numismatic Guaranty Company - NGC)

- 1955 TDR PROOF - This nickel has a special error called "Tripled Die Reverse". This means that the back side of the nickel was struck three times, creating a triple image.
- 1955 D/S - This nickel has an error where the "D" mint mark was stamped over an "S".

1955 D over S nickel (Images provided by Numismatic Guaranty Company - NGC)

- 1956 QDR - This nickel has a special error called "Quadrupled Die Reverse". This means that the back side of the nickel was struck four times, creating a quadruple image.
- 1956 TDR - This nickel has a special error called "Tripled Die Reverse". This means that the back side of the nickel was struck three times, creating a triple image.

1956 triple die reverse nickel (Images provided by
Numismatic Guaranty Company - NGC)

- **1957 QDO PROOF** - This nickel has a special error called "Quadrupled Die Obverse". This means that the front side of the nickel was struck four times, creating a quadruple image.
- **1958 D/INVERT D** - This nickel was made at the Denver Mint in 1953 and has an error where the "D" mint mark is doubled with the second "D" being upside down.
- **1960 QDR PROOF** - This nickel has a special error called "Quadrupled Die Reverse". This means that the back side of the nickel was struck four times, creating a quadruple image.
- **1964 TDR PROOF** - This nickel was produced with a special process in the Proof format and has a special error called "Tripled Die Reverse". This means that the back side of the nickel was struck three times, creating a triple image.
- **1964 DDO** - This nickel was produced with a doubled-die error at the Philadelphia Mint, resulting in a coin with two images.

1964 double die nickel (Images provided by
Numismatic Guaranty Company - NGC)

- 1964 D/D - This nickel was produced with an error where the "D" mint mark was stamped over a "D".
- 1968 S DDO PROOF - This nickel was produced with a doubled-die error at the San Francisco Mint in the Proof format and has a special error called "Doubled Die Obverse". This means that the front side of the nickel was struck twice, creating a double image.
- 1971 S DDR PROOF - This nickel was produced with a double-die error at the San Francisco Mint in the Proof format and has a special error called "Doubled Die Reverse". This means that the front side of the nickel was struck twice, creating a double image.
- 1971 NO "S" PROOF - This nickel was produced without the "S" mint mark at the San Francisco Mint in the Proof format.
- 1975 D MISPLACED MINT MARK - This nickel was produced with a misplaced mint mark at the Denver Mint.

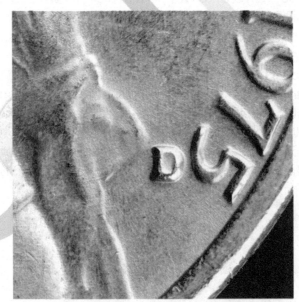

1975-D misplaced mint mark nickel (Images provided by Numismatic Guaranty Company - NGC)

- 1990 S DDO PROOF - This nickel was produced with a doubled-die error at the San Francisco Mint in the

Proof format and has a special error called "Doubled Die Obverse". This means that the front side of the nickel was struck twice, creating a double image.

- 2004 P HANDSHAKE DDO - This nickel was produced with a doubled-die error at the Philadelphia Mint, resulting in a coin with two images.

2004-P Handshake double die nickel (Images provided by Numismatic Guaranty Company - NGC)

Dimes

- 1946 DDO - This error occurs when the design on the coin is doubled, resulting in a second, slightly offset image on the obverse (front) of the coin.

1946 double die dime (Images provided by Numismatic Guaranty Company - NGC)

- 1946 DDR - This error occurs when the design on the coin is doubled, resulting in a second, slightly offset image on the reverse (back) of the coin.

- 1946 D/D – This error has an error where the "D" mint mark was stamped over an "D".

1946 D over D dime (Images provided by Numismatic Guaranty Company - NGC)

- 1946 S/S - This error has an error where the "S" mint mark was stamped over an "S".
- 1946 S/S/S/S - This error has an error where the "S" mint mark was stamped over an "S" four times over.
- 1946 S/S - This error has an error where the "S" mint mark was stamped over an "S."
- 1946 S/S/S - This error has an error where the "S" mint mark was stamped over an "S" three times over.
- 1946 S/S - This error has an error where the "S" mint mark was stamped over an "S."
- 1947 DDO – This error occurs when the design on the coin is doubled, resulting in a second, slightly offset image on the obverse (front) of the coin.
- 1947 S/D SANS SERIF - This error was produced in 1947 and features the "S" mint mark and "D" mint mark, both with a sans serif font.

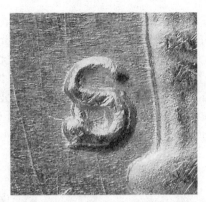

1947 S over D Sans Serif dime (Images provided
by Numismatic Guaranty Company - NGC)

- 1947 S/D TRUMPET S - This dime features the "S" mint mark and "D" mint mark, with the "S" mint mark having a trumpet font.
- 1947 S/S - This dime features two "S" mint marks, indicating it was struck at the San Francisco Mint.
- 1947 S DDR - This dime features a doubled die reverse, with a second, slightly offset image of the design on the reverse of the coin.
- 1948 DDR - This dime features a doubled die reverse, with a second, slightly offset image of the design on the reverse of the coin.

1948 double die reverse dime (Images provided
by Numismatic Guaranty Company - NGC)

- 1948 S/S - This dime features a doubled "S" mint mark.
- 1950 DDR PROOF - This dime is a proof coin that features a doubled die reverse, with a second, slightly offset image of the design on the reverse of the coin.
- 1950 D DDR - This dime features a doubled die reverse, with a second, slightly offset image of the design on the reverse of the coin.

1950-D double die reverse dime (Images provided by Numismatic Guaranty Company - NGC)

- 1950 S/INVERT S - This dime features doubled inverted "S" mint mark, with the "S" appearing upside down.
- 1950 S/S - This dime features a doubled "S" mint mark.
- 1951 D/D - This dime features a doubled "D" mint mark.
- 1953 D/HORIZ D - This dime features a doubled "D" mint mark that is horizontal, instead of being struck vertically like the standard issue dimes.
- 1953 S/S - This dime features a doubled "S" mint mark.

1953 S over S dime (Images provided by Numismatic Guaranty Company - NGC)

- 1954 DDO PROOF - This dime is a proof coin that features a doubled die obverse, with a second, slightly offset image of the design on the obverse of the coin.
- 1954 DDR - This dime features a doubled die reverse, with a second, slightly offset image of the design on the reverse of the coin.
- 1954 S/S - This dime features a doubled "S" mint mark.
- 1954 S NO "JS" - This dime does not feature the "JS" initials of the designer, John Sinnock, on the reverse of the coin.
- 1955 S/S - This dime features a doubled "S" mint mark.
- 1956 DDO PROOF - This dime is a proof coin that features a doubled die obverse, with a second, slightly offset image of the design on the obverse of the coin.
- 1959 D/INVERT D - This dime features an inverted "D" mint mark, with the "D" appearing upside down.
- 1959 D/D - This error has an error where the "D" mint mark was stamped over an "D."

1959 D over D dime (Images provided by Numismatic Guaranty Company - NGC)

- 1960 DDO PROOF - This dime has a doubled die error in proof form.
- 1960 DDR PROOF - This dime has a double die error in proof form.
- 1960 D/D - This error has an error where the "D" mint mark was stamped over an "D".
- 1961 D DDR - This dime has a reverse double die error.
- 1962 D/HORIZ D - This dime has a double die error with the "D" being horizontal over a "D."
- 1962 D/D - This error has an error where the "D" mint mark was stamped over an "D".
- 1963 DDR PROOF - This dime has a reverse double die error in proof form.
- 1963 DDO - This dime has an obverse double die error.

1963 double die dime (Images provided by Numismatic Guaranty Company - NGC)

- 1963 DDR - This dime has a reverse double die error.

1963 double die dime (Images provided by
Numismatic Guaranty Company - NGC)

- 1963 D/D - This error has an error where the "D" mint mark was stamped over an "D."
- 1963 D DDR - This dime has a reverse double die error.
- 1964 DDO BLUNT 9 PROOF - This dime has a double die error with a blunt 9 in proof form.

1964 double die blunt 9 proof dime (Images provided
by Numismatic Guaranty Company - NGC)

- 1964 POINT 9 - This dime has a different 9 than the standard issue, with a pointed 9 instead of a blunt 9.
- 1964 BLUNT 9 - This dime has a blunt 9 instead of a pointed 9.

- 1964 DDR BLUNT 9 - This dime has a double die error with a blunt 9.
- 1982 NO P – This dime is missing the 'P' mintmark on the obverse side of the coin, which was accidentally omitted during the minting process.

1982 "no p" dime (Images provided by Numismatic Guaranty Company - NGC)

- 2004-D GOUGE – This dime is featuring a long, shallow gouge on the reverse side of the coin, caused by a heavy object or foreign material striking the die during the striking process.

2004-D die gouge dime (Images provided by
Numismatic Guaranty Company - NGC)

Quarters

- 1964 D DDR - This quarter is a reverse doubled die error,
  meaning that the design elements on the coin appear to
  be doubled or overlapping.

1964 double die reverse quarter (Images provided
by Numismatic Guaranty Company - NGC)

- 1964 D TYPE C REV OF 65 - This quarter has a Type C reverse, meaning that the reverse design of the coin was changed in 1965.
- 1965 DDO - This quarter has a doubled die obverse, meaning that the design elements on the front of the coin appear to be doubled or overlapping.

1965 double die quarter (Images provided by Numismatic Guaranty Company - NGC)

- 1965 DDR - This quarter is a reverse doubled die error, meaning that the design elements on the coin appear to be doubled or overlapping.
- 1966 DDR - This quarter is a reverse doubled die error, meaning that the design elements on the coin appear to be doubled or overlapping.
- 1968 S DDO PROOF - This quarter is a proof coin that was struck from specially prepared dies and intended for collectors and has a double die obverse error.
- 1968 S/S PROOF - This quarter is a proof coin that was struck from specially prepared dies and intended for collectors. This quarter has an error where the "S" mint mark was stamped over an "S."
- 1968 S DDR PROOF - This quarter is a proof coin that was struck from specially prepared dies and intended for collectors and had a double die reverse error.
- 1968 D DDR - This quarter is a doubled die error, meaning that the design elements on the coin appear to be doubled or overlapping.

1968-D double die reverse quarter (Images provided
by Numismatic Guaranty Company - NGC)

- 1970 S DDR PROOF - A proof quarter with a "S" mint
mark and showing a double die reverse error.
- 1970 D DDO - A quarter with a "D" mint mark and showing a double die obverse error.

1970-D double die quarter (Images provided by
Numismatic Guaranty Company - NGC)

- 1970 D DDR - A quarter with a "D" mint mark and showing a double die reverse error.

1970-D double die reverse quarter (Images provided
by Numismatic Guaranty Company - NGC)

- 1971 DDR - A quarter showing a double die reverse error.

1971 double die reverse quarter (Images provided
by Numismatic Guaranty Company - NGC)

- 1971 D DDR - A quarter with a "D" mint mark and showing a double die reverse error.
- 1776-1976 S SILVER DDO PROOF - A proof quarter
made of silver and showing a double die obverse error.
- 1776-1976 D DDO - A quarter with a "D" mint mark and
showing a double die obverse error.

1976-D double die quarter (Images provided by
Numismatic Guaranty Company - NGC)

- 1969 S DDO PROOF - This quarter is a proof coin that
was struck from specially prepared dies and intended for
collectors and has a double die obverse error.
- 1969 S/S/S PROOF - This quarter is a proof coin that
was struck from specially prepared dies and intended
for collectors. The "S/S/S" means that the coin has triple
struck "S."

- 1969 D/D - This error has an error where the "D" mint mark was stamped over an "D".
- 1983 P SPITTING EAGLE - This quarter error refers to a 1983 Philadelphia minted quarter that features a design of a spitting eagle on the reverse. This error is caused by a misalignment of the reverse die during the striking process, resulting in the eagle appearing to spit.

1983-P "Spitting Eagle" quarter (Images provided by Numismatic Guaranty Company - NGC)

- 1990 S DDO PROOF - This quarter error refers to a 1990 San Francisco minted proof quarter that has a doubled die obverse.
- 2004 EXTRA LEAF - This quarter error is a rare and valuable variety that affects the reverse of the Wisconsin State Quarter, featuring an additional leaf on one of the corn stalks, caused by an extra impression from the die during the minting process.

2004 "Extra Leaf" quarter (Images provided by
Numismatic Guaranty Company - NGC)

- 2009 DISTRICT OF COLUMBIA DDR - This quarter error refers to a 2009 District of Columbia quarter that features a doubled die reverse.

2009 double die reverse quarter (Images provided
by Numismatic Guaranty Company - NGC)

- 2015 HOMESTEAD DDR - This quarter error refers to a 2015 Homestead National Monument of America quarter that features a doubled die reverse.

2015 Homestead double die reverse quarter (Images provided by Numismatic Guaranty Company - NGC)

Half Dollars

- 1964 ACCENT HAIR PROOF - This error has an unusually pronounced hairline on Lady Liberty.
- 1964 ACCENT HAIR DDO PROOF - This error that has an unusually pronounced hairline on Lady Liberty and is a doubled die obverse.
- 1964 ACCENT HAIR QDR PROOF - This error has an unusually pronounced hairline on Lady Liberty and is a quadrupled die reverse.
- 1964 TYPE 1 REVERSE STRAIGHT "G" - This error has a straight "G" in "God" on the reverse side.
- 1964 DDO PROOF - This is a doubled die obverse proof.
- 1964 QDR PROOF - This error is a quadrupled die reverse proof.
- 1964 TDO PROOF - This error refers to is a tripled die obverse proof.
- 1964 DDO - This error is a doubled die obverse.

1964 double die half dollar (Images provided by
Numismatic Guaranty Company - NGC)

- 1964 DDR - This error a doubled die reverse.
- 1964 D DDO - This error is with a doubled die reverse.
- 1964 D TDO - This error is a tripled die obverse.
- 1964 D QDO - This half dollar features a quadruple die reverse.

1964-D quadruple die half dollar (Images provided
by Numismatic Guaranty Company - NGC)

- 1964 D/D - This half dollar is a "D" over "D" error.

1964 D over D half dollar (Images provided by
Numismatic Guaranty Company - NGC)

- 1964 D/HORIZ D - This half dollar features a horizontal "D" mintmark, which is a result of an extra punch being applied at an angle instead of vertically.
- 1965 SMS DDR PROOF - This half dollar is a proof coin that was struck in 1965 as part of the Special Mint Set program. It features a doubled die error, resulting in doubled design elements on the coin.
- 1965 DDR - This half dollar features a doubled die reverse.

1965 double die reverse half dollar (Images provided by Numismatic Guaranty Company - NGC)

- 1966 SMS NO "FG" - This half dollar is a coin that was struck in 1966 as part of the Special Mint Set program, and it is missing the "FG" initials that were normally included on the coin's design.
- 1967 SMS NO "F" - This half dollar is a coin that was struck in 1967 as part of the Special Mint Set program, and it is missing the "F" initial that was normally included on the coin's design.
- 1968 S SERIF S/KNOB S PROOF - This half dollar is a proof coin that was struck in 1968 and features an error variation, where the "S" mintmark has a doubled knobbed appearance.
- 1968 S INVERTED S PROOF - This error is a proof half dollar from 1968 with the letter "S" on the reverse side of the coin with an extra inverted "S".

- 1968 S DDR PROOF – This error is a proof double die reverse.
- 1970 S DDO PROOF - This error is a proof double die obverse.
- 1971 S DDO PROOF - This is another example of a proof half dollar with a doubled die obverse error.
- 1971 D DDO - This an error with a doubled die obverse error.
- 1972 DDO - This is an error with a doubled die obverse error.
- 1972 D NO "FG" - This is a half dollar without the initials "FG" (Frank Gasparro) on the reverse side of the coin.

This 1977-D half dollar is missing the designer's initials (Images provided by Numismatic Guaranty Company - NGC)

- 1977 D DDO - This is a half dollar with a doubled die obverse error.

1977-D double die half dollar

- 1982 P NO "FG" - This is a half dollar without the initials "FG" on the reverse side of the coin.
- 1983 P NO "FG" - This is another example of a half dollar without the initials "FG" on the reverse side of the coin.
- 1988 S DDO Proof - This is a proof half dollar with a doubled die obverse error.
- 1988 P NO "FG" - This is a half dollar without the initials "FG" on the reverse side of the coin.
- 1992 S DDO SILVER PROOF - This is a silver proof half dollar with a doubled die obverse error.
- 2018 S Silver Light Finish Reverse Proof Set - This is a set of silver half dollars from 2018 with a light finish reverse proof error. The set includes proof versions of the half dollar with a light finish on the reverse side of the coin.

Dollar Coins

- 1971 S DDO SILVER TYPE PROOF - This error has a doubled die obverse error. The "S" on the coin indicates that it is a proof coin struck at the San Francisco Mint. The "TYPE PROOF" is a reference to the fact that this particular coin is a type of proof.
- 1971 S DDO SILVER PROOF - This coin is a proof dollar has a doubled die obverse error. The "S" on the coin indicates that it is a proof coin struck at the San Francisco Mint.

1972-S double die silver proof dollar (Images provided by Numismatic Guaranty Company - NGC)

- 1971 S TDO SILVER PROOF - This coin is a proof dollar with a tripled die obverse (TDO) error.
- 1971 S SILVER "PEG LEG" - This coin is a dollar with a design error that results in one of the legs of the eagle on the reverse of the coin appearing shorter than the other.
- 1971 S DDR SILVER PROOF - This coin is a proof dollar with a doubled die reverse error.
- 1971 D FRIENDLY EAGLE - This coin is a dollar with a design error that results in the eagle on the reverse of the coin appearing in a more relaxed or "friendly" position compared to the typical design.
- 1971 S SILVER "PEG LEG" - This coin is a dollar with a design error that results in one of the legs of the eagle on the reverse of the coin appearing shorter than the other.
- 1971 S/S SILVER - This coin is a dollar with a doubling error on both the mint mark a S over S error.

1971 S over S dollar (Images provided by Numismatic Guaranty Company - NGC)

- 1972 S DDO SILVER PROOF - This coin is a proof dollar with a doubled die obverse error.

- 1972 TYPE 1 - This is a reference to the different design types of the dollar coins produced in 1972.
- 1972 TYPE 2 - This is a reference to the different design types of the dollar coins produced in 1972.

1972 Eisenhower dollar types (type 1-left, type 2-middle, type 3-right) (Images provided by Numismatic Guaranty Company - NGC)

- 1972 TYPE 3 - This is a reference to the different design types of the dollar coins produced in 1972.
- 1972 D DDR - This coin is a dollar with a doubled die reverse error.
- 1972 D DDO & DDR - This coin is a dollar with both a doubled die obverse and a doubled die reverse error.
- 1973 S DDR CLAD PROOF - This coin is a proof dollar with a doubled die reverse error. "CLAD" means that it is a clad coin (consisting of a sandwich of copper between two layers of nickel).
- 1776-1976 S TYPE 1 CLAD PROOF - This is a proof version of the 1976 Bicentennial Silver Dollar, which was struck using a special die. The Type 1 variety is characterized by a wide space between the letters of "Liberty" on the obverse.
- 1776-1976 S TYPE 2 CLAD PROOF - This is another proof version of the 1976 Bicentennial Silver Dollar, which is similar to the Type 1, but has a narrow space between the letters of "Liberty."
- 1979 P NARROW RIM - This is a 1979 Susan B. Anthony dollar coin with a narrow rim, which is different from the normal issue with a wider rim. This is common and holds no value past face value.

73

1979 narrow rim dollar (Images provided by
Numismatic Guaranty Company - NGC)

- 1979 P WIDE RIM - This is the normal issue of the 1979
  Susan B. Anthony dollar coin, which has a wider rim than
  the Narrow Rim variety. This is the scarcer design.

1979 wide rim dollar (Images provided by
Numismatic Guaranty Company - NGC)

- 2000 P CHEERIOS PROMOTION - This is a special edi-
  tion of the "golden" dollar that was produced for a promo-
  tional giveaway by the Cheerios cereal brand.
- 2000 P PROTOTYPE REVERSE - This is a rare version
  of the 2000 dollar that features a different reverse design
  than the standard issue.
- 2000 P SPEARED EAGLE - This is a 2000 dollar that features a misaligned strike on the reverse, which gives the
  appearance of a spear passing through the eagle's wing.

2000 "Speared Eagle" dollar (Images provided by
Numismatic Guaranty Company - NGC)

This is our list of specific dates are just a few examples of the many rare and valuable errors that exist in US coinage.

Although we couldn't provide images for all the errors we have mentioned, we'd like to show you how to extract the text from this book using your mobile device so that you can see the images of coins we couldn't provide photos of. First, you will need to go to the Google Images website (images.google.com) on your device's web browser. Then follow these steps:

1. Tap the camera icon in the search bar to open the "Search by Image" screen.
2. If you have a picture of the book's text on your phone, you can select the "Upload an image" tab and choose the image from your photo library.
3. Once you have selected the image, tap "Search" to upload the picture to Google Images.

4. Google will display the results for that image, including any text that it recognizes within the image. Look for the text you want to search for in the search results.

5. Tap on the "Google Search" button next to the text you want to search for. This will open up the Google Search page with the search term already entered in the search box.

6. The search results page will display on your device, and you can browse the results on either an Apple or Android device.

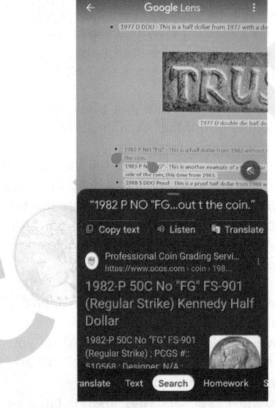

Example of Google image for text highlighting

By using your phone to extract text from this book, you can quickly and easily research coin errors. Use this book as a reference guide to help you identify and analyze coin errors in your collection.

Recap of Coin Errors

In this book, we've explored the fascinating world of coin errors. From pennies to quarters, we've covered a wide range of errors that have been produced over the last 100 years. We've seen that errors can occur due to a variety of reasons, such as double striking, omitted mint marks, and design doubling. These errors offer a unique window into the production process and the technology available at the time, and they are highly sought after by collectors.

A Look into the Future of Coin Errors

As technology continues to advance, it's safe to say that the production of coins will become even more precise. However, mistakes and errors will always be a part of the production process. After all, humans are involved, and we all make mistakes from time to time. So, while the frequency of errors may decrease, they will never completely go away.

The world of coin errors is a fascinating one, filled with rare and valuable finds. Whether you're a beginner or an experienced collector, there is always something new to discover. So, keep an eye out for those unusual coins in your change, who knows, you might just find the next big coin error. And remember, always have a sense of humor about it, collecting should be fun and not too serious! After all, my name is CoinHub.

Buy, Sell, Go Live!

Get a free $15 credit on Whatnot to start your coin collection today.

CHAPTER 9: SELLING COIN ERRORS: THE ART OF LETTING GO

Coin collecting can be an enjoyable hobby, but sometimes you reach a point where you want to sell your errors to make room for new additions or simply to make some extra cash. Selling coin errors is not as simple as just listing them on eBay and waiting for the bids to roll in. In order to sell your errors successfully, you need to understand the market and know how to present your coins in the best light. Here are some tips for selling coin errors:

Know Your Coins: Before you even think about selling your errors, you need to know what you have. Research each coin and understand its value, rarity, and historical significance. A coin that is worth $10 to one collector might be worth $1,000 to another, so it's important to have a good understanding of what you're selling.

Choose Your Platform: There are many ways to sell coin errors, including online marketplaces like eBay, Whatnot, forums, social media groups dedicated to coin collecting, and local coin shows/shops. Consider your options and choose the platform that works best for you.

Present Your Coins Well: When it comes to selling coin errors, presentation is everything. Make sure your coins are well-protected and take high-quality photos to showcase their unique features. Be sure to include a detailed description of the coin and any relevant information that will help a potential buyer understand why it's special.

Be Realistic About Price: It's tempting to ask for top dollar for your errors, but you need to be realistic about what the market will bear. Do some research to see what similar coins are selling for and be prepared to negotiate on price.

Utilize Social Media: In today's world, social media is a powerful tool for selling anything, including coin errors. Utilize platforms like Instagram, TikTok, and Facebook to showcase your errors and reach a wider audience. You can even create your own coin-focused social media account, like CoinHub! We will talk about this more next.

Now, let's talk about the art of letting go. It can be tough to part with coins that you've put time, money, and energy into collecting, but sometimes it's necessary. And remember, just because you're selling a coin doesn't mean you have to say goodbye to it forever. You might even be able to buy it back later.

Selling coin errors can be a fun and lucrative way to turn your hobby into cash. Just make sure you know your coins, choose the right platform, present them well, be realistic about price, and utilize social media to reach a wider audience. And most importantly, have fun with the process!

CHAPTER 10: THE POWER OF SOCIAL MEDIA IN COIN COLLECTING

Coin collecting has been a popular hobby for centuries, but with the rise of social media, it has become even more accessible and exciting for people of all ages. The world of coin collecting is no longer just limited to dusty old books and quiet auction houses. Now, it's a vibrant and thriving community of passionate collectors and enthusiasts, all brought together by the power of social media.

Social media has revolutionized the way we communicate, share information, and connect with one another, and the world of coin collecting is no exception. One of the best things about social media and coin collecting is the sense of community it creates. No longer do you have to feel like you're the only one who loves the thrill of finding a rare coin in your pocket change. With social media, you can connect with a global community of collectors and enthusiasts, sharing your finds, asking for advice, and learning from others.

And let's not forget about the entertainment factor. Social media has given coin collectors a new platform to showcase their finds and share their knowledge with the world. From TikTok coin hunt challenges to Instagram unboxing videos, there's no shortage of creative and engaging content being produced by coin collectors.

In the midst of all this social media activity, I'd like to give a shoutout to CoinHub, my own coin social media platform! Whether you're just starting out as a collector or you're a seasoned pro, CoinHub is the place to be for all things coin related. From live videos and educational videos to fun challenges and exciting finds, we've got it all. And with a growing community of passionate collectors, you'll never feel like you're alone in your coin collecting journey. So be sure to follow us on TikTok (@coinhub) and Instagram (@coinhubs) to stay up-to-date on all things coin collecting!

In conclusion, the influence of social media on coin collecting has been tremendous, bringing together a global community of collectors and enthusiasts and providing a platform for them to connect, share, and learn. So if you're a coin collector, embrace the power of social media and join the conversation. The future of coin collecting rests in the hands of social media!

COIN GLOSSARY

- ANA - American Numismatic Association
- AU - About Uncirculated
- BN - Brown
- BU - Brilliant Uncirculated
- CAC - Certified Acceptance Corporation
- CC - Carson City
- CDN - Coin Dealer Newsletter
- CH - Choice
- CN - Copper Nickel
- COA - Certificate of Authenticity
- COPY - Counterfeit
- C/N - Clad Nickel
- DDR - Doubled Die Reverse
- DDO - Doubled Die Obverse
- DMPL - Deep Mirror Proof-Like
- EF - Extremely Fine
- F - Fine
- G - Good
- HAW - High End About Uncirculated
- IGC - Independent Grading Company
- Luster - Refers to the surface shine of a coin
- MS - Mint State
- NGC - Numismatic Guaranty Corporation
- PCGS - Professional Coin Grading Service
- PF - Proof
- PL - Proof-Like
- PMD - Post Mint Damage
- PR - Proof

- Red - Refers to a coin that has not been circulated and still has its original red color
- RPM - Repunched Mint Mark
- VF - Very Fine
- XF - Extremely Fine

These terms are commonly used in the coin collecting community and can help you understand the condition and grade of a coin. Understanding these terms is important for buying and selling coins, as the grade of a coin can greatly impact its value.

ABOUT COINHUB

As the founder of CoinHub, I am humbled and grateful for the journey that has brought me to where I am today. It all started on January 22, 2020, when I was inspired by my mother to create a TikTok and Instagram page to share my passion for modern U.S. coin errors and their values. I never could have imagined the impact that my simple idea would have on my life and the lives of others.

In my first month of posting videos, I was amazed to see 20,000 followers and video views quickly grow to over 2 million, respectively. However, I soon realized that I needed to focus on personal matters and took a break from producing new content.

But the coin collecting community wouldn't let me stay away for long. In August of 2020, I posted a video about a Coca-Cola bottle cap coin produced in Fiji and was blown away by the response. The video garnered over a quarter-million views and tripled my follow count to 60,000. By October of that same year, CoinHub had grown to over 300,000 followers and 75 million video views on TikTok alone.

In June of 2022, I was honored to sign a partnership deal with WhatNot Inc to promote their new coin auctioning platform. The support and success of CoinHub allowed me to incorporate the company as CoinHub Media and move the company to Lebanon, Ohio in November of 2022.

Today, I am happy to say that CoinHub has a following of over 1.5 million on TikTok, Instagram, and Facebook, with over 200 million video views. I am grateful for each and every one of my followers and for the opportunity to share my love for coin collecting with others.

As a Christian, I believe that all things are possible through God and that He has a plan for each and every one of us. I am thankful for the opportunities and blessings that have come my way through CoinHub and I will continue to strive to use my platform for good and to bring joy and education to others.

THE STORY BEHIND COINHUB'S FOUNDER

Blake Alma is a young individual who discovered his passion for the outdoors at the age of 12. Since then, he has turned his love for the outdoors into a successful multimedia lifestyle. Blake had made a name for himself in the outdoor community by showcasing his outdoor experiences and accomplishments through various platforms such as TV, social media, and digital content creation.

Blake's journey started when he was just a young boy growing up in the countryside. He was always fascinated by the natural world around him and had a desire to explore and discover everything it had to offer. At the age of 12, Blake started to take his love for the outdoors to the next level by participating in hunting and fishing trips with his family and friends. He quickly realized that his passion for the outdoors was something special, and he wanted to share it with the world.

Blake started to document his outdoor experiences through social media and quickly gained a following of people who were also passionate about the outdoors. He began to create content that showcased his outdoor adventures, including hunting trips, fishing expeditions, and camping trips. Blake's unique perspective on the outdoors and his infectious personality quickly made him a popular figure in the outdoor community.

Blake's success on social media led him to become an outdoor advocate and personality, and he soon landed his own TV show on the Hunt Channel. The show, called The Outdoor Experience, showcased Blake's love for the outdoors and allowed him to share his experiences with a wider audience. Blake's show was well-received by viewers, and he quickly became one of the most recognizable faces in the outdoor community.

In August of 2018, Blake Alma stepped down from his role as an outdoor advocate and personality. Blake had gained recognition for his outdoor achievements at a young age, and it had become a defining part of his identity. However, after working in the industry for 4 years, he noticed a shift in the reactions to his work. As he grew older, he experienced more hateful and godless opposition, rather than a loving and accepting outdoor community. This, along with his fleeing youth, led him to resign from hosting The Outdoor Experience and his other outdoor roles.

As of February 2022, Blake now resides in Lebanon, Ohio and still has a love for the great outdoors, particularly fishing. In January 2020, he started a new venture, a coin collectors blog called CoinHub, where he discusses all things coins and precious metals on several different social platforms.

Today, he is a 22-year-old entrepreneur who has been fortunate enough to make a contribution to the coin collecting industry. As a young boy of 12, Blake developed a love for the outdoors and coin collecting, which eventually evolved into a career. Through his creation of CoinHub, Blake aimed to provide a platform that connects coin collectors and enthusiasts from around the world and creates a sense of community within the industry.

Blake attributes his success to his strong Christian faith, which has guided him in all aspects of his life, including his work in the coin collecting industry. Although Blake has gained recognition for his knowledge and expertise in coin collecting, he considers himself to be a humble student of the industry and always strives to learn more. He is grateful for the opportunity to share his insights and advice with collectors of all levels of experience, through his work with CoinHub and his presence on social media platforms such as TikTok, Facebook, and Instagram.

Blake's contributions to the coin collecting industry have been acknowledged by the media, including several news articles, like in the *New York Post* and *Fox Business*, where he offered his thoughts on determining the value of coins. However, Blake is quick to acknowledge that his success is largely due to the support and encouragement of the coin collecting community, as well as his faith in God.

Blake Alma is a soft-spoken but dedicated entrepreneur who has made a small yet meaningful contribution to the coin collecting industry. He is grateful for the opportunity to serve the coin collecting community through his work with CoinHub and his social media presence. Blake is always striving to learn more and improve, and he looks forward to continuing his journey in the fascinating world of coin collecting.

Made in the USA
Las Vegas, NV
02 September 2023

76965486R00056